# 100 Flowers
## ADULT COLORING BOOK

Special Art

# The Preview Page:

# JOIN OUR FACEBOOK GROUP WHERE YOU CAN SHARE YOUR ARTWORKS!

**FACEBOOK GROUP:**
Special Art - Artwork

SCAN ME

THE BEST WORKS WILL BE PUBLISHED ON THE OFFICIAL INSTAGRAM ACCOUNT :

**INSTAGRAM :**
@Specialart_coloring

VISIT OUR WEBSITE TO RECEIVE THE **GIFT** SURPRISE THAT WE HAVE PREPARED FOR YOU!

Special Art

SCAN ME

WEBSITE:
www.SpecialArtBooks.com

# THANK YOU SO MUCH FOR PURCHASING THIS BOOK.

Thank you... because **YOU**
give colour and life to our Books...

.. And so we have prepared
**A GIFT** for you!

To get it, use the camera of your phone
to scan the **QR CODE**
on the next page.

We look forward to see you
in our **BIG FAMILY**
of colour lovers.

Good Colouring

# GET YOUR GIFT!
## OUR 100 BEST COLORING PAGES

Do you have a question or concern? Write to us.
www.specialartbooks.com | support@specialartbooks.com

# This Book Belongs To:

_____

Special Art

Choose the colors you love,
Find your favorite drawing
to start with...
And give it life!

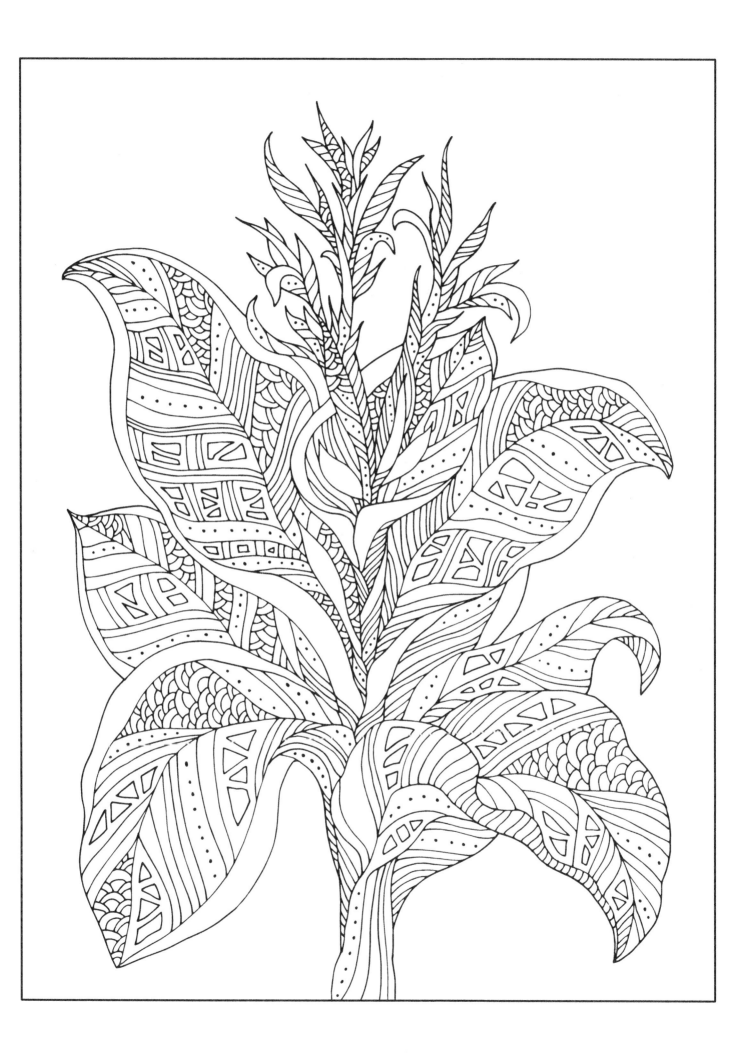

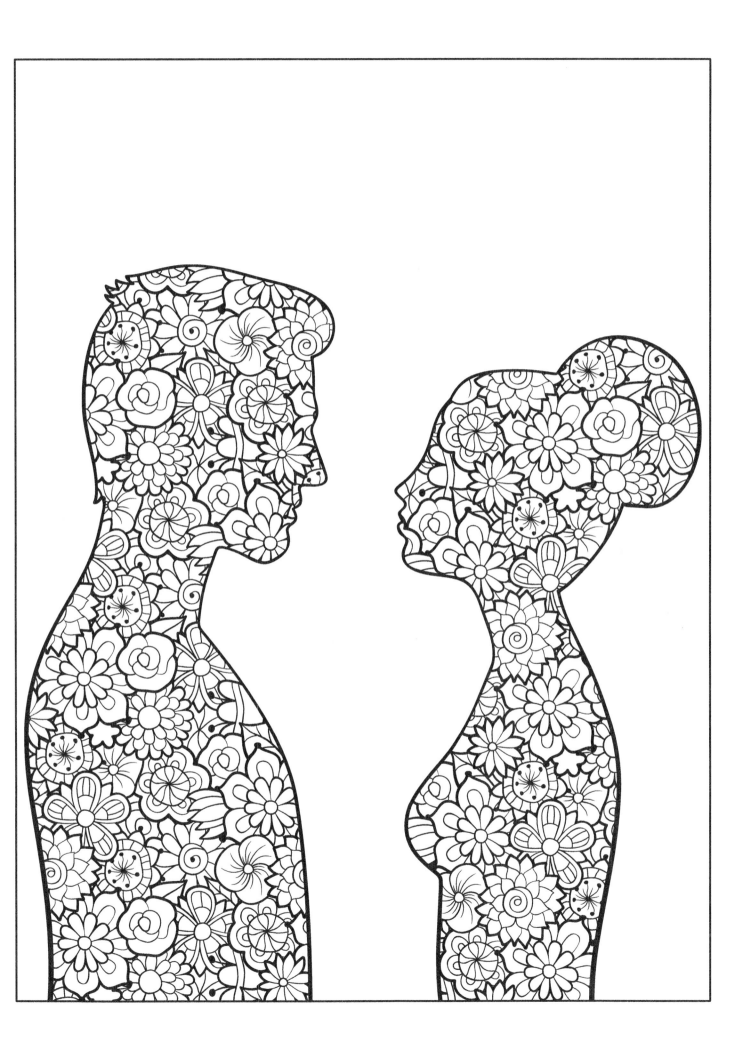

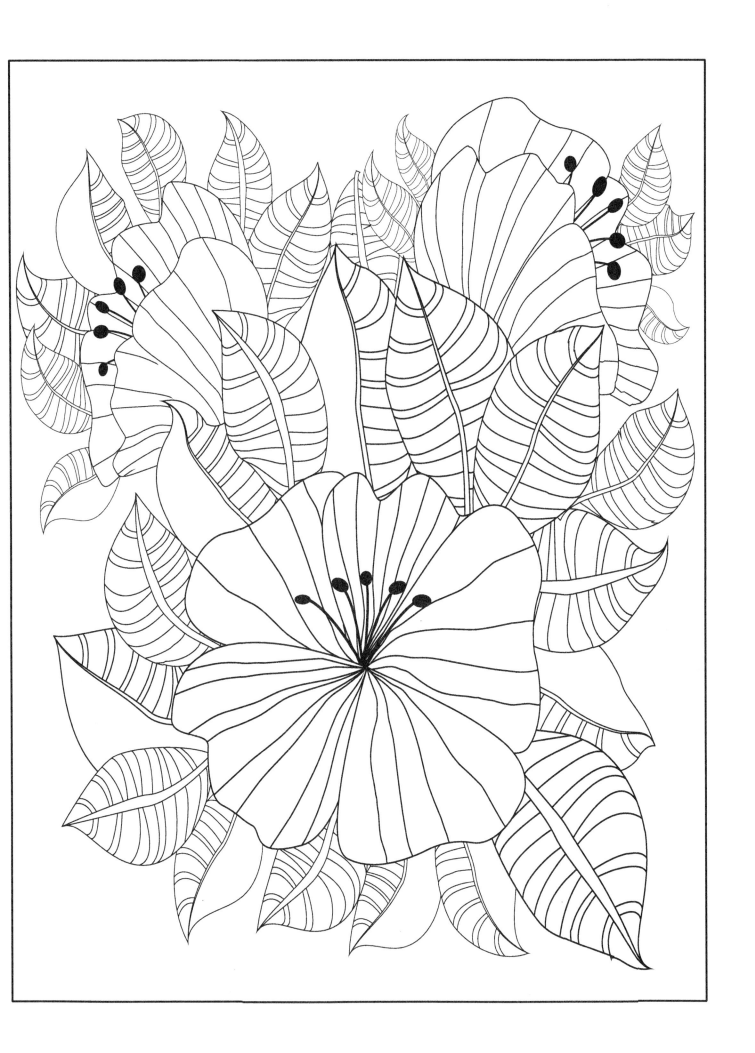

# IF YOU LIKED THIS BOOK, HELP US LEAVING A <u>REVIEW</u> ON <u>AMAZON</u> !

**1.** Go to Amazon from your profile and click on "My orders"

**2.** Search this book

**3.** Click on "Write a review for this product"

**4.** Leave us your rating and if you want, add some photos of your fantastic achievements!

## <u>QUICK SOLUTION</u>:
### SCAN YOUR COUNTRY QR CODE BELOW

*SCAN ME*

| UK | US | CANADA |

## THANK YOU VERY MUCH FOR YOUR SUPPORT!

# JOIN OUR FACEBOOK GROUP

✔ Community of Colourists from around the World
✔ Get Free Member-only Content
✔ Share your Artwork
✔ and much more !

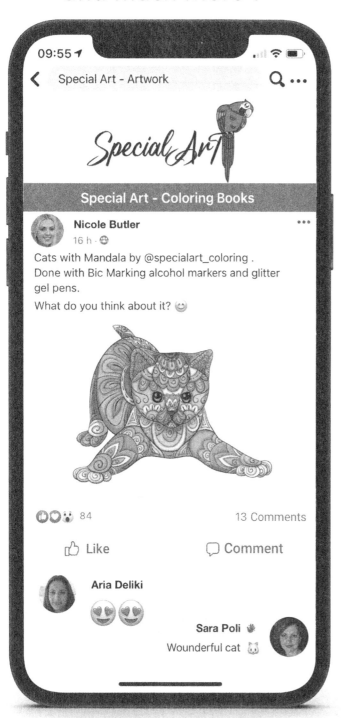

## ENTER NOW

**1.**
Search the group on Facebook:
Special Art – Artwork

**2.**
Join the Group

**3.**
Answer welcome questions

**4.**
You are now part of the community

## OR SCAN WITH YOUR MOBILE PHONE CAMERA
## THE QR CODE BELOW

# FOLLOW US ON INSTAGRAM

✓ To share your artwork with us
✓ See your masterpieces shared on our account
✓ Keep up to date with Contests and News
✓ and much more !

## FOLLOW US NOW

### 1.

Search on Instagram :
@specialart_coloring

### 2.

Follow us

### 3.

Send us a message with photos
of your creations

## TO FIND US IMMEDIATELY SCAN WITH YOUR MOBILE PHONE CAMERA THE QR CODE BELOW

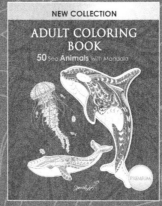

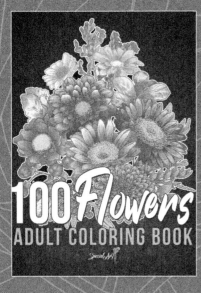

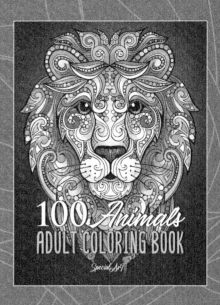

# News

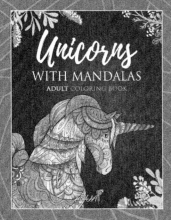

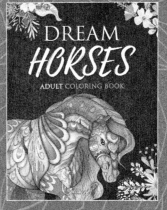

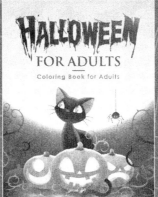

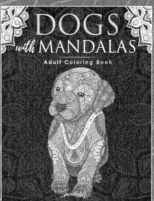

# Children's Books

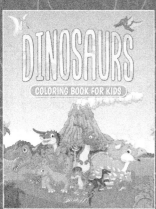
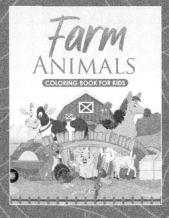
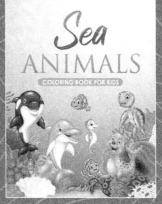

# WE HOPE YOU ENJOYED THIS BOOK!

## Digital Shop
### START YOUR COLORING ADVENTURE

You can find the digital version of this title and many more digital releases on :

## WWW.SPECIALARTBOOKS.COM/SHOP

*SCAN ME*

THANK YOU VERY MUCH FOR CHOOSE ONE OF OUR BOOKS!

Printed in Great Britain
by Amazon